DISCOVERING GOD'S WILL AND WAY

by

Darrell Huffman

25 24 23 22 21 20   1 2 3 4 5 6 7 8

DISCOVERING GOD'S WILL AND WAY–
Copyright ©2020 Darrell Huffman

Published by:
Emerge Publishing, LLC
9521B Riverside Parkway, Suite 243 Tulsa, Oklahoma 74137
Phone: 888.407.4447   www.EmergePublishing.com

Library of Congress Cataloging-in-Publication Data:
ISBN: 978-1-949758-894 Perfect Bound
Also available in audiobook on www.audible.com

INTRODUCTION

To be successful in this life we must always follow the example of the Lord Jesus. When the Lord walked among us in His earthly ministry, He taught the people by both precept and example. His faith was strong and His words were filled with power because He was completely submitted to being one with His Father in fulfilling His will on earth.

In John 8:28,29, the Lord Jesus reveals two great foundation truths that gave Him success in all He did.

> "Then Jesus said to them, "When you lift[a] up the Son of
> Man, then you will know that I am *He,* and *that*
> I do nothing of Myself; but as My Father taught Me,
> I speak these things. [29] And He who sent Me is with Me.
> The Father has not left Me alone, for I always do those things
> that please Him." John 8:28,29 NKJV

These two great truths are: The Lord Jesus always acted on God's Word and He always did His works in the way that pleased His Father. When we discover God's will, that is found in His Word, then allow the Holy Spirit to lead us in the way we are to do it, we too will begin to see the same mighty results in our lives that we read about in the Bible.

3

God is no respecter of persons. These truths will work for all who find them and put them to work in their lives. These two keys to strong faith are discovering God's will and God's way to do it. To do this we must receive the revelation of God's Word and be led by the Holy Spirit on how to do it.

It is the purpose of this book to help you to discover God's will and God's way so that you can follow Jesus' example in your walk of faith; always doing those things which are pleasing to Him.

CHAPTER ONE

"And since we have the same spirit of faith, according to what is written, 'I believed and therefore I spoke,' we also believe and therefore speak" (2 Corinthians 4:13 NKJV).

The apostle Paul is writing this to the church. He had just written in verses 3 and 4 that if the gospel is hidden, it's hidden to them that are lost, those whose minds have been blinded by the god of this world. Satan is constantly working against people to try to keep them from knowing the truth of the Lord Jesus Christ. You may have found out that even after you got saved, the devil still tried to work against the knowledge of the Lord to keep you bound.

If the devil cannot stop you from getting saved, he tries to stop you from having an effective walk for God until you go to heaven someday. The devil will surrender you going to heaven, but he hates for you to have success on the way. But aren't you glad Jesus didn't just save us to go to heaven someday? He saved us so we could walk in the power of God here on this earth and be difference makers in this life.

I've told people jokingly that if you just get saved to go to heaven, then when you get baptized, we ought to pray an extra long prayer when we're holding you under the water. We won't say amen until you quit bubbling. We'll just send you right on to heaven. We wouldn't get many people baptized that way. So we don't get saved just to go to heaven. We get saved because Jesus is real, and deep down we understand that we need to come out of darkness into light and make Jesus our Lord.

We got saved to live for God. We got saved to serve the Lord. We were brought out of the kingdom of darkness, Colossians 1 says, and brought over into the kingdom of the son of God. He "qualified us to be partakers of the inheritance of the saints in the light" (v 12 NKJV). You know what has to happen before you're going to partake of your inheritance? You have to know what the inheritance is and how to get it. The blessings of the Lord do not fall upon you like ripe cherries falling off of a tree. You have to shake the tree to get the cherries to fall. We have to learn how to operate in the things of the kingdom of God, and here Paul says, "and since we have the same spirit of faith, according to what is written, 'I believed and therefore spoke,' we also believe and therefore speak. " (2 Corinthians 4:13 NKJV).

Paul is talking to us about how faith works, and notice he starts off by saying, we have the same spirit of faith. That excites me. I have the same spirit of faith. How did I get it? Romans 12:3 (NKJV):

> "For I say, through the grace given to me, to everyone
> who is among you, not to think *of himself* more highly
> than he ought to think, but to think soberly, as
> God has dealt to each one a measure of faith."

God has given us a measure of faith. You may wonder: when did He give it to me? Ephesians 2:8 says you're saved by grace through faith. So when did God give you your faith? When you got saved. Brother Hagin tells a story of when somebody came up to him and said, "Pray for me so that I'll have faith." He said, "Then just get saved." Because if you get saved, you have faith because you have to get saved by faith. God gives you the faith to get saved so you can walk in His grace. God gives you the measure of faith when you're born again.

Peter also had something to say about the same measure of faith that God's dealt to each and every one of us.

> "Simon Peter, a bondservant and apostle of Jesus Christ,
>
> To those who have obtained like precious faith with us
> by the righteousness of our God and Savior Jesus Christ"
> (2 Peter 1:1 NKJV).

Notice that before Peter declared his function, he declared who he was. You'll never function in your ministry until you become a servant of the Lord Jesus Christ, because He's the one you're serving through your ministry. The word apostle was Peter's title, it was his job description, but a bond-servant was who he was. Now a bondservant was one who willingly indentured themselves to someone else. They were not taken captive. They were not made to serve. They willingly chose to submit to that person and serve them. Peter was saying, I have willingly submitted myself to be a servant of the Lord Jesus Christ. Because I have set myself not to serve me, but to serve Him, He has made me an apostle. In other words, He's given me this function in the kingdom of God.

Then he addresses those who have been saved. Those who have been dealt the measure of faith, those who had the same spirit of faith. What he is saying here is you and I have the same kind of faith the apostles had. We have received the same, "like precious faith" the apostle Peter had. So whatever the apostles had, we have; whatever they did, we can do. My faith is not less than theirs, and their faith is not greater than mine.

In fact, some translations say faith of "equal value" (NABRE and LEB). I have obtained faith of the same value that God gave to the apostles. They could turn cities upside down and shake nations. You and I should be able to turn cities upside down and shake nations. Your faith wasn't just given to you so you could be blessed and go to heaven. Your faith was given to you so you can make a change in your environment and so that you can be an influencer of the kingdom of God in your sphere of influence. If we'll learn how to operate in that same spirit of faith, we could use our faith to move mountains, we could pray down the power of God, we could use our faith and set people free. We could use our faith and get people healed; we could use our faith and release the kingdom of God and loose the power of God to move so that God will be glorified and not the devil. It is important for you to understand that God has given you the same precious faith, the same faith of value that He gave to the apostles. You have it. What you have to do is learn how to use it.

There are two key truths in 2 Corinthians 4:13 that, if you're going to walk in the spirit of faith, you're going to have to get a hold of. The first one is that we have a spirit of faith "according to what is written." I believe you have to build your faith on the written Word of God. I believe based on the Word, not based on what I feel, not based on what I see, not based on the opinion or the fad that's going around at the time. The apostle Paul says that just as they believe what was written, we also have to believe what's written. You have to get into the Word of God and find out the knowledge of God's will. Because if you don't know what God's will is, you can't operate in it. Your faith will never rise above the level of your revelation, your knowledge of God's Word. You can't believe for something you don't know.

How can you get this word in you? Let's look at Psalm 119. God is speaking here through David:

"The entrance of Your words gives light;
It gives understanding to the simple"(v 130 NKJV).

Notice it doesn't say the word gives light, but it is the word that enters in you that gives you light. If I don't let it enter into me, it doesn't bring any light to me. As 1 John 2 says, if you don't have His light, you're walking in the darkness. You don't know where you're going. You're going to stumble around and you're not going to get anywhere (see verses 9-11). Until I allow the Word of God to have entrance into my life, I'm walking in darkness. I'm stumbling around. I'm not going to get anything. Even though it's mine, I can't get it because I don't know it. The Word not only gives us light, it gives us understanding. All of a sudden the Word comes alive to you and you think, "Oh yeah, I get that. I understand that now." That word went from written in the Bible to entering into you as a rhema Word from God. It brought the light of God's will into your life.

"So then faith comes by hearing, and hearing by the word of God" (Romans 10:17 NKJV).

"And He said to them, 'He who has ears to hear, let him hear!'" (Mark 4:9 KNJV).

We have to hear the Word of God, not just listen to it. And those who hear will be given more. The more I allow God to speak into me, the more God will speak into me, but I have to get it in me.

Now look at another verse in Psalm 119.

"Your word is a lamp to my feet
And a light to my path" (v 105 NKJV).

The Word is God giving me direction for my life. The Word is God revealing His will for me in my life. When you get right down to it, there are two W's in faith. And the first w of faith is knowing God's will, and you can't know God's will unless you know God's Word because God's Word is God's will.

The first step of me walking in the spirit of faith is believing according to what it is written. In other words, I let the written Word come into my heart and bring understanding of God's will in my life. For example, I can never believe God for healing until 1 Peter 2:24 enters into me. Then all of a sudden it begins to speak to me and get me understanding that by the stripes that wounded Jesus, I was healed. That begins to jump out to me. As another example, I'm going to walk in poverty and I'm going to be frustrated all the time, if Philippians 4:19 does not enter into me and bring light that God will supply all that I need.

One of the greatest things that ever entered in my life was
John 10:10 (NKJV):

"The thief does not come except to steal, and to kill, and to
destroy. I have come that they may have life, and that they
may have *it* more abundantly."

That was one of the greatest revelations. It entered into me. I
grabbed a hold of that real quick because up until that time, I
questioned God. I didn't know if it was God that was doing it
to me because I was raised up more in religion. They believed
in God, but they didn't know much about Him. I went to a
church where they'd shout and carry on but I didn't know
what they were shouting about. We loved the people and
appreciated what they had, but we were taught the Lord gives
and the Lord takes away (see Job 1:21). We were kind of
taught that God would bless you, then to keep you humble,
He'd take it back. Like, God gave you a new car then
somebody would come along and steal it, to keep you
humble. Or He gets you ready for a race and makes you sick
so you'd be humble when you couldn't run in it. I just
thought if it was a good day, God was doing something good
for me. If it was a bad day, God had some problem with me.
Then somebody came along and preached John 10:10. I
thought, "My God, the devil has been doing that to me all
these years."

I heard Brother Copeland share a story of when he was preaching in a theater back in the early days. He'd been preaching on salvation authority, and a security guy working there got saved on a Wednesday night. Then on Friday night, Brother Copeland got into teaching on John 10:10. As he was preaching, he heard a commotion behind the curtain. Somebody was just stomping and cussing. Several ushers ran over and quieted it down. He went ahead and finished his service. Afterward, the security guy walked over with a sheepish look on his face. He said, "Brother Copeland, I need to apologize to you. All that cussing and carrying on, that was me." He said, "I thought you got saved. Why'd you cuss and carry on?" The guard said, "The devil's a thief that comes to steal, kill, and destroy and it just made me so mad. He'd been robbing me all those years. I thought I'd just give him a good cussing." His motive was good, but his method wasn't quite right.

But we ought to get that mad. Not to cuss, but that mad that we're not going to let the devil steal from us anymore. The only way he's going to keep stealing from you is if you don't know what the Word says, so you have to get in the Word. Paul says, "According to that which is written, we believed," but it has got to go beyond written.

"Therefore *it is* of faith that *it might be* according to grace, so that the promise might be sure to all the seed, not only to those who are of the law, but also to those who are of the faith of Abraham, who is the father of us all (as it is written, 'I have made you a father of many nations') in the presence of Him whom he believed—God, who gives life to the dead and calls those things which do not exist as though they did" (Romans 4:16, 17 NKJV).

I want you to see a couple of things about Abraham's faith. He starts off with the written word. Notice that when God gives you the word, He gives you the outcome and not the process. God spoke to Abraham and told him what he was to be. He didn't necessarily give him the process, He gave him the final outcome. God says by His stripes, you were healed. God doesn't say, "You're sick, but you'll get healed." God says, "The Word says this is where you're to get to. This is your hope. This is your goal. This is your vision." The Word is showing that God calls the end from the beginning. In other words, He doesn't start in the beginning. He starts at the end. When you read the Word, the Word tells you who you are as the end result.

"Therefore, if anyone *is* in Christ, *he is* a new creation; old things have passed away; behold, all things have become new" (2 Corinthians 5:17 NKJV).

He doesn't tell you the process of getting there. He just says you will get there. The Word tells us God's will.

Now look what Paul went on to say of Abraham:

> "who, contrary to hope, in hope believed, so that he became the father of many nations, according to what was spoken, 'So shall your descendants be'" (Romans 4:18 NKJV).

In verse 17, he said "according to what is written." But here he says "according to what was spoken." So God's written word went from a word he read in the Bible to a word that was real in his heart. It became his word. It became a spoken word from God. In other words, I have to get into His written word until the Holy Ghost speaks it into me and it becomes a spoken word from God to me. Then even though it looks hopeless, my faith will still be in God. I'll still have hope and expectation because I've got a word spoken to me from God's Word. It's written right here, and God will do what He said He would do. So you see the words spoken become God's will operating in my life.

> "And not being weak in faith, he did not consider his own body, already dead (since he was about a hundred years old), and the deadness of Sarah's womb" (Romans 4:19 NKJV).

Abraham received the entrance of God's word into his heart. And that word went from written to spoken, and it gave him an understanding that God had a divine plan for his life. And it was God's will for him and his wife to have children and descendants and build a great thing for God. He might have been thinking: "God has spoken His will into my life. And though it looks like it won't work, I'm going to take my eyes off of what doesn't look like it'll work. I put my eyes on what God said will work. Instead of being moved by the problem, I'm going to be moved by the word of God because I'm going to keep believing and speaking the word, not believing and speaking the problem."

"He did not waver at the promise of God through unbelief, but was strengthened in faith, giving glory to God, and being fully convinced that what He had promised He was also able to perform" (Romans 4:20-21 NKJV).

Everything Abraham is doing is based on God's promise or God's word to him. We can do the same thing. Paul told the Corinthians every promise of God is yes and amen to us (see 2 Corinthians 1:20). If you want to find God's will and how to get it into your life, find what's written and stay with it. Let the spirit of God open it up to you until it begins to speak to you, and let it enter into your heart. You know when it's entered into your heart when it brings light. All of a sudden instead of me walking around in the darkness, wondering what I'm going to do, I've got a word down inside of me. That word is: it's God's will for me to come out of this thing.

So look what Abraham did because he's got that spoken word. He was strong in faith and was persuaded that God could do as He promised. Now, how did he get to that place where he became fully convinced and persuaded that God would do that for him? That word had gone from a written word to a spoken word. It went from just the logos to the rhema, and it became God personally speaking to him. He understood that if God said it, God will do it because God cannot lie. God is faithful to His promises and God will do this. Now all of a sudden, Abraham knows the will of God. He found the will of God in this situation through the written word of God and he stayed in it until it became God speaking to him.

God will never speak contrary to His Word. You may come to me and say, "Well, the Lord told me this, this, and this." But if I can take you to the Bible passage that contradicts that, then the Lord didn't speak to you. That's how you try the spirits. Like John said in 1 John 4, you have to try a spirit because if it's not speaking in line with the Word of God, it wasn't God talking to you. God's Word is forever settled in heaven. He isn't going to change it. Not one jot nor one tittle (see Matthew 5:18). It's there and that written word was written for our sakes so that we can know God's will for our lives. So the first step of your faith working is this: you're going to get into God's Word and find out the will of God, according to the Word of God. You're going to stay with it until it enters into you and brings light. It will get you out of the darkness of confusion, doubt, and fear.

If somebody comes to you and says, "How can you believe God that's going to happen?" You know it's because you got a word for it. That word's down on the inside of you, and every time you get to thinking about something different, God's word just comes up. You've got something to hang on to, and you're going to praise God when you can't see it out here. We'll praise God because we've got His promise. Whenever we can't feel it, we will praise God because we got His promise, and His Word is working mightily in us. I know it's God's will to heal me. It's God's will to deliver me. It's God's will to get me through this situation. It's God's will to make me the head and not the tail. It's God's will to make me above and not beneath. It's God's will to bless me coming in and bless me going out. It's God's will to cause my enemies to turn and run from me. It's God's will to bless all the work of my hands. It's God's will to prosper me and bless my home and bless everything around me. It's in Deuteronomy 28, and it just jumped off the pages and became real in my life.

But knowing God's will is only half of the equation to have successful faith. Once you know His will, you have to put the second w and that is this: His way. You're going have to find out His way to do His will. Most believers are not getting defeated because they don't know God's will; they're getting defeated because they haven't found out the way God wants to do His will in that situation. People have heard the Word. Most of us are not getting defeated because we don't know the will of God, but it's because we haven't taken time to find out the way God wants to do it. The two W's of faith are the will of God and the way of God.

Let's go back to 2 Corinthians 4:13:

> "And since we have the same spirit of faith, according
> to what is written, 'I believed and therefore I spoke,'
> we also believe and therefore speak" (NKJV).

Notice this: You have to have the spirit operating along with the Word to have the spirit of faith. If you don't have the spirit of God working with the Word of God, then you have the letter of the law, but you don't have the spirit of the law. The letter kills, but it's the spirit that brings life to the Word.

> "For as many as are led by the Spirit of God,
> these are sons of God" (Romans 8:14 NKJV).

You probably know this Scripture, but let's look at it in light of walking in faith and using our faith. Notice that as sons and daughters of God, we're supposed to be being led by the spirit of God. To be led means He's leading the way, He's directing the way, He's the pathfinder. The Holy Spirit has been sent from God to lead you in the way God wants you to go. If we're being led by the Spirit of God, we're the sons of God. The next verse sheds light on how the Holy Spirit leads us.

"For you did not receive the spirit of bondage again to fear, but you received the Spirit of adoption by whom we cry out, 'Abba, Father'" (Romans 8:15 NKJV).

I don't have to be afraid to follow the Holy Spirit. I need to be confident that the Holy Spirit is going to lead me in the way that I need to go to do what God's called me to do. When I cry out, "Abba, father," then God, my Father, is speaking into me through the Holy Spirit and showing me the way that I'm supposed to go.

"The Spirit Himself bears witness with our spirit that we are children of God" (Romans 8:16 NKJV).

When the Holy Spirit is leading you, He doesn't lead you by feelings. He doesn't lead you by the flesh. He leads you by your spirit. That leading has to come from down on the inside, meaning you have to be led by your spirit. That's being led by the Holy Spirit and not led by what your mind is telling you or how you think you should do it.

We'll read a verse like "by whose stripes you were healed" and then immediately we'll run off in our minds and think, "I'm just going to go get healed." You should have stopped and said, "Now, Holy Spirit, how do you want me to use 1 Peter 2:24 to get my healing? Show me. You want me to apply this Scripture in my life. I know it's your will. Now show me the way I'm supposed to go with this to make it work in my life."

"But the Helper (Comforter, Advocate, Intercessor—
Counselor, Strengthener, Standby), the Holy Spirit,
whom the Father will send in My name [in My place,
to represent Me and act on My behalf], He will teach
you all things. And He will help you remember everything
that I have told you" (John 14:26 AMP).

The Holy Spirit is your strengthener. The Holy Spirit's always the one standing by to help you out. The Holy Spirit has come in Jesus's place to act on His behalf and do for us what the Lord would do if He was here Himself. That means I need to give a lot of respect to the Holy Spirit whenever He begins to witness in my spirit as to what I need to do because He's not representing Himself. He's here in the Lord's place, the same as if Jesus was there telling me to do that. Look again at what the Holy Spirit is going to do with that unction and leading and representing the Lord. The Holy Spirit is now going to do for you and me what the Lord Jesus did when He was here with the disciples; the Holy Spirit is going to show us where to go, how to do it, how to talk, how to confess it, how to apply the Word in our life. He's going to teach us these things by bearing witness and leading us in our spirit.

"But when He, the Spirit of Truth (the Truth-giving Spirit) comes, He will guide you into all the Truth (the whole, full Truth). For He will not speak His own message [on His own authority]; but He will tell whatever He hears [from the Father; He will give the message that has been given to Him], and He will announce *and* declare to you the things that are to come [that will happen in the future].

He will honor *and* glorify Me, because He will take of (receive, draw upon) what is Mine and will reveal (declare, disclose, transmit) it to you" (John 16:13-14 AMP).

When the Spirit comes, He will guide us into truth. Remember in John 17: 17 Jesus said we could be sanctified with truth, and His Word is truth. So we could say it like this: When the Spirit of the Word comes, He's going to guide you in the full knowledge and the truth of the Word of God. In other words, He's going to take the Word from a written word, and He's going to bring a revelation of it into your heart and make it truth operating in your life. He's going to reveal it as a spoken word of God. When that word becomes a spoken word to you, it becomes the truth that now is controlling your life. That truth controls your actions. It controls your attitude. It controls your confession. It controls what you're believing, and the Holy Spirit is going to bring that truth to you.

Next, Jesus said in John 16 that the Spirit will tell us what He hears from the Father. He says He will find out what the Father wants you to do and bring that revelation to you. Then you can go do what God wants you to do and the way He wants you to do it. So why is it the spirit of faith? Because the Holy Spirit takes the written word and makes it truth and reveals it to us. Then the Holy Spirit takes the way that God wants you to use that truth and leads you and guides you and shows you how to make it work in your life.

What I begin to find here is that faith is no longer steps one, two, and three. Faith is no longer just a legalistic thing. Faith is not of the letter; faith is a spiritual force. It's a spirit of faith and it comes straight from God. The Holy Spirit guides us into the truth of the word and that word then becomes a revelation, a rhema word from God. Then the Holy Spirit takes that word and takes the will of the Father and begins to guide us and show us how to make it work in our lives.

Just because somebody else used their faith one way to get something doesn't mean you can just follow them and go do the same thing. They did it because God told them to do it that way. Now what you need to do is get in God's presence and find out how God wants you to do it. God may tell you to do it exactly like they did, but you're not doing it because they did it. You're doing it because you got in the presence of God, and God spoke His word in your spirit. The Holy Spirit then begins to lead you. You step out on that truth and do it the way God told you to do it. When you do God's will and you're doing it God's way, God makes it happen in your life.

Most of us are being defeated because we don't take time once we've heard God's will to find out how God wants us to do it in our life. You have to be led by the Spirit on the way of God, just like you have to be led by the Spirit to get in the Word of God.

"But ye have an unction from the Holy One, and ye
know all things" (1 John 2:20 KJV).

Many translations say you have an anointing from the spirit. It's also known as the witness of spirit. It's so important that you follow the witness of the Spirit in your faith. You cannot use your confession and override the unction of the Holy Ghost. You cannot use your faith or confession and override the leading of the Holy Spirit.

I remember the story Brother Hagin taught years ago: There was a couple who were both ministers. They came to a meeting with him, and he taught them about being led by the Spirit. They came up to him after and said they wished they'd have heard this a year ago. The man said, "About a year ago, my wife and I had to go to the next town about an hour and a half away. I had my devotions. I prayed, felt good in my spirit. We had breakfast and went out to get in the car. And just as I sat down in the car in the driveway, I felt this in my spirit, 'Wait ten minutes; don't leave right now. Just wait 10 minutes.'

"I looked at my wife and said, 'Well, I just believe God.' We prayed in Jesus's name. I bound the devil. I thanked the Lord for His safeties. And we just took off. We were about halfway there. And we came around a curve. There had been an accident. I couldn't stop. I plowed right into the car. Before we could get out of the car, a truck came and plowed into the rear of my car. My wife was in the hospital for weeks. It almost killed us. If we'd have just listened to that witness down in the Spirit and sat there that ten minutes, it would have kept us out of the entire accident." But he was a faith person. He knew it was God's will to cover him and protect him. And he knew no weapon formed against him shall prosper (see Isaiah 54:17), but no weapon formed against you will prosper if you listen to God and not go where that weapon can get you.

We have to learn in walking this faith walk that, first, you have to get into the Word and let the Word enter into you and become light and revelation.

"If you abide in My word, you are My disciples indeed.
And you shall know the truth, and the truth shall make
you free" (John 8:31-32 NKJV).

If I want to be discipled, I've got to get in the Word until it becomes the truth. It will burn like a branding iron in my heart that I know that I know that I know that I know. Then I know that I know that I know that this is God's will in my life, but I'm only halfway there now. Then I need to pray in tongues and worship God and seek the Lord until the unction of the Holy Ghost rises up. The Holy Ghost will say, "That's my will. Here's how you do it." Because now I've not only got His will, I've got His way to do it. When I'm doing God's will God's way, God comes through. I'll win.

David says something in Psalm 25 that just jumps out and goes right along with this idea.

> "Show me Your ways, O Lord;
> Teach me Your paths.
> Lead me in Your truth and teach me,
> For You are the God of my salvation;
> On You I wait all the day" (Psalm 25:4-5 NKJV).

Notice David is putting both of these principles in there. He asks the Lord to teach him. In other words, I need to know your will. But then he asks God, "Show me your ways." I looked up the word "ways" in the Hebrew. It means a course or mode of action. David was saying, "Lord, teach me what your will is. And then show me the course or mode of action I'm to take to make it work in my life."

Let me give you a couple of examples. First is 2 Kings 5:1-15, about Naaman, the Syrian general. The army had captured a young Hebrew girl, and they brought her back and she is working with Naaman's wife in his home. Though he was a mighty man, he was a leper. The servant girl says, "If my master was just over in Samaria, there's a prophet over there. God would heal him if he just got over to that prophet." So he goes to the king of Syria. The king says, "Great. If I can get my general healed, let's go." He sends the king of Israel a letter. He says, "I'm sending Naaman my great general to you so that you can heal him of his leprosy." And the King of Israel says, "Oh my God." Because he can't heal him. Of course, Elisha, the prophet, says, "Send him over here. There's no problem." Naaman knows it is God's will to heal him.

He goes over there in his chariot and all of his horses and all of his soldiers and uses all of his pomp and ceremony because he's this big guy. Elisha turns to his servant and says, "Tell him to go out and dip himself seven times in the river Jordan and he'll be healed." The guy goes out and he says, "Mr. Super-duper, I'll tell you what you do. The prophet said, here's the way God's going to heal you. You go down to the Jordan, wash yourself seven times, and when you come up, you'll be healed."

Naaman got mad. He went into a fit of rage. He says, "I just knew—I had it figured out in my head that that man was going to come out here and wave his arms and lightning was going to flash in the power of God, and in a boom— hallelujah—I was going to be healed." He had his own way of getting his healing. He already figured it out in his head. He gets mad and turns his chariot around, and he's heading back home. Finally, one of his lieutenants looks at him and says, "Listen, if he told you to go out and do something great, you would have done it. I want you to just go down and jump in the river seven times; come on, man."

Naaman decided to obey God's way and went down to the Jordan. He jumped in, washed and on the seventh time he came out, the leprosy was gone. God's will was done God's way. It got him a miracle. But he had to have God's way. He knew God's will. But if he hadn't found out God's way and obeyed it, it would have never happened for him. You can't make God's will conform to your way. You have to take God's will and let it conform you to His way, which means you're totally submitted to His will and His way of working it out in your life. That's the spirit of faith.

I'll show you another story from 1 Chronicles 14:8-17. David has now been anointed king of Israel, and the Philistines hear about it. They're all aggravated because David had this big reputation and now he is the king. They decide they're going to come up against him. They come up on the mountain, and David is so smart. David inquires of the Lord, "Shall I go out and pursue them?" God says to pursue them. David has God's will. Now he's got God's way. He goes right out there and defeats the Philistines.

Then the Philistines regrouped and came up through the valley. Most of us would have said, "We know it's God's will to defeat the Philistines, and we're just going to go. We don't even need to pray. We know what God will do. Let's just go get them." But David inquires of the Lord again. It's the same enemy that's come back, but he doesn't go on the first prayer. He's now praying again. He asks if they should go and pursue. But God says, "No, not at this time. Go out around the mulberry trees. When you hear the wind blowing like a troop marching through, know that I've given them to you." And David goes out and obeys. Same enemy, two different ways to defeat him.

Just because you got healed one way once before doesn't mean you can make that same way work every time. What's the way God's wanting to do it now? Sometimes God's way is to go get some help. We faith people think we can't ever go to a doctor. I've known faith people that died knowing it was God's will to heal them, but His way was to go get some medical help because God was going to work that way to get them through it but they didn't go.

In John 9, Jesus finds a blind man. Jesus spits on the ground, makes some clay, and puts it in his eyes. Then He says, "Now go over and wash in the pool of Siloam and you'll be healed." Why did He do it that way? He's God; why didn't He just lay hands on him? God's will is to heal that blind man. But His way is for him to go to the pool and wash his face. God's will is to heal you. Maybe it's God's way to send you to a doctor, show you what's wrong, and help you to get some victory in that situation. Maybe it's God's will to heal you and He's already shown it to you. Maybe His way is for you to have hands laid on you, or maybe it's His way for you to be annointed with oil or maybe His way is for you to just speak

29

it out yourself. Maybe it's His way for you to fast for a little bit. Maybe it's His way for you to have someone agree with you. Maybe it's His way for you to have someone else pray for you.

You have to find His way every time that the enemy comes against you. You can't just go after Him with the way you did it last time. Every time, you need to have a revelation from God. You may have whipped this enemy three or four times before, but this time is different. You need to find out how God wants you to do it this time. We're to be those who are being led by the Spirit every day; He will lead us in every situation that we face. If we're going to walk in victory, especially during this time we're in, we're going to have to get in God's Word and take that written word and stay with it until the Holy Spirit speaks it into us. We let the Holy Spirit enter it into our hearts, and it begins to bring light. All of a sudden, we no longer doubt that God wants to do this. We got a word. We know it's His will. Just like Abraham, it doesn't matter what it looks like. It doesn't matter what it feels like. It doesn't matter what anybody else is saying. My hope is established on the will of God. I'm going to praise God and stay with God until God shows me the way I am supposed to do this. When I lock in on His way, nobody's going to talk me out of it. Nobody's going to shame me from it.

I've always walked in health. God has blessed me and helped me. I appreciate all the healings that I've gotten over the years. There were times I prayed, but I want to tell you about a time a few years ago. I was actually down in Mexico. I was going to try to get a workout in between some other activities. I sat down on a bench and put a little bit of weight on to loosen up. I got about five reps in, and I got my arms up partway, and the right shoulder just quit. When I played ball years ago, I hurt that shoulder and I had to rehab it. Over the years, it would get sore and I could rehab it. Sometimes I'd walk into the weight room, and I'd put five pounds on this arm. I could do the normal on the other one, but I'd work it back up. I was always able to pray, believe, use my faith, and get it done. But this time, it wasn't working. The more I prayed, the more I believed, the more I did what I've always done, it just kept getting worse.

Then finally, three months later, I had a friend of mine come in, and he'd had a shoulder separation and a torn rotator. He started telling us about the situation and all the pain. It was Sunday morning, but after the service, we go back home and Bonnie said, "Your going into the doctor. Because he just explained and described your pain. I live with you and at nighttime you roll over groan in your sleep. I know you've gotta be hurting." It did, it was hurting. I'd been confessing the Word every day and it's hurting. So finally I said, "Lord, what do you want me to do?" I wish I had done that three months before. I knew it was His will to heal me. I can quote you healing Scriptures until the cows come home. I build them into my spirit.

I finally just said, "Lord, what would you have me to do?" He said, "Go get your shoulder checked." So I called the doctor up, and immediately, they had an opening. So I went, they did all their stuff, and the doctor comes and says, "You've got a torn rotator. Now we can help you with therapy or we can fix it." I said, "Fix it." Was it God's will to fix it? He wouldn't have told me to go have it checked if it wasn't His will to fix it. They said, "Okay, we're going to set you up to bring you in and do the surgery." I prayed this: "Lord, here's what I'm believing. If it's your way for me to get this shoulder healed by going to this doctor and having this surgery, then I believe you for a tremendously successful surgery. I believe you that you're going to make it quick and good, no complications. Then I'm going to come out of there and recover so fast there'll be a testimony of your miracle power to the people that are working with me." We set it up, and I went in, and they did the surgery.

When they come back out, the surgeon told my wife, "It's amazing. His shoulder was a whole lot worse than we thought. He had little bone spurs. That's why it wouldn't heal itself because bone spurs had developed over the years. Every time he'd move his arm a certain way, they cut into that ligament and tear it again. So we had to go in and clean off the bones spurs. Then we had to repair the torn rotator. .But you know what? We got done about twenty minutes quicker than we thought we would. It was amazing how smooth it went."

They put me in this sling, and this is when I came up with this message. I was going to preach Sunday morning with my arm in a sling. I went back to the therapist seven days later, and I had a golf shirt on. He says, "We'll come back here and we're going to examine the rotation." So we go back and I just took the sling off, lay it down, dropped my arm, reached up to unbutton, pulled the shirt up and over my head, then lay there. And he looked at me; he was getting ready to help me. He said, "What'd you do?" I said, "You told me to take this shirt off. I had to take the shirt off." He said, "You can't take your shirt off. It's too early. Your arm doesn't work. You can't do that." I said, "Well, it did." He said, "Do that again." I said, "What, this?" He said, "Yeah, you can't do that."

In seven days, I was back to eighty percent rotation movement in all directions. I went to three therapies, and after the third therapy, I went back to the surgeon. I had a hundred percent movement. He said to go to this last therapy and tell him the doctor released me. I went to the therapist. He said, "You're a freak of nature." I said, "No, I'm a believer that trusts God. I did it God's way, and God just gave me my miracle."

Somebody might wonder if I believe that was God's best. Yes, that was God's best. That was His way. And I did it. In fact, that shoulder is stronger than the other shoulder. It worked because I took time to not only find God's will, but to find God's way of doing it. When I taught that, it released everybody. In the faith movement, we think we have to get it by confession only or by standing and believing and never putting anything practical to it. But God is a God of spiritual and practical. You need to get free from everybody else's opinion. You get free from what everybody else thinks. You get in the presence of God and you find God's will in His Word. Then let the Holy Spirit show you how to make it work in your life. And then you do it. I don't care what anybody else thinks. It's better to be healed than it is to be thought well of by other people.

If we learn this and we walk in this, faith is going to rise up and be mighty in our lives again. Maybe you have been struggling with this. You know it's God's will to do something. He spoke it into your heart, but you don't know the way He wants to do it. You can't just do it the same way every time. Just like David, same enemy, but there are two different ways to defeat him. Same will, but two different ways. You need to find what God's will right now is and what's His way of doing it.

If you are ready to commit yourself and consecrate yourself in this, use this prayer:

"Lord, no longer my will. No longer my way, but Lord, from this moment on, I open my heart up. Holy Spirit, I ask you to bring me into the will of God, the knowledge of the truth of God. Lord, I believe you right now to begin an unction in me to show me the very way that you would have me to do this. Show me the way, show me how I'm to pray and how

I'm to go about it and how I'm to get the thing done. Because Lord, the how and the way is just as important as the will. Lord, I just set myself never to be just presumptuous of thinking, 'we did it this way before so we'll do it again.' But in every situation that I face, help me to stop and seek you for your will and your way so that you are leading me in every situation. And Lord, I just put you out in front of me. You're the great shepherd. And I right now open my heart up and believe that you will begin to speak to me and make clear not only your will, but the way to get it done. Show me the pathway, the mode, the course I'm to follow. And I just open my heart up and receive it right now. I receive it right now."

Then begin to thank the Lord. Let the entrance of His Word give you light and understanding, and then let the Holy Spirit begin to witness to your spirit. What's that unction saying to you? What's the witness of the Spirit telling you to do about that thing? Just submit to God and just yield to God. That's faith. Faith is you trusting God and doing it His way following after His will.

Every successful ministry has found not only God's will for their ministry, but the way God wanted them to do it. Every successful couple not only found God's will for their lives, but the way to make that marriage work. Every family that's raising their kids and seeing success with their kids, they know God's will to raise them. Then God shows them the way they're supposed to do it because every child is different and you have to learn how to minister to each child according to their personalities. Every witness, every evangelism is successful by learning that it's God's will to save the lost, but then finding the way for each and every individual they speak to. Everybody's different and you can't just witness the same way to everybody. In every situation, we have to learn the way of the Spirit so that we're operating in the spirit of faith and not just a knowledge of faith, not just in the letter, but in the spirit of faith. Then we're walking with God.

CHAPTER TWO

"Therefore know that *only* those who are of faith are
sons of Abraham. And the Scripture, foreseeing that
God would justify the Gentiles by faith, preached the
gospel to Abraham beforehand, *saying,* 'In you all the
nations shall be blessed.' So then those who *are* of faith
are blessed with believing Abraham.

"For as many as are of the works of the law are under the
curse; for it is written, 'Cursed *is* everyone who does not
continue in all things which are written in the book of the
law, to do them.' But that no one is justified by the law in the
sight of God *is* evident, for 'the just shall live by faith.'"
Galatians 3:7-11 (NKJV)

In the previous chapter, we looked at 2 Corinthians 4:13 and
we found out that faith is a spiritual law, not just a formula.
Faith has to have the Spirit of God involved in it. If faith isn't
alive, it is just a ritual. If faith isn't a living thing on the inside
of you, it's just a legalistic way of living without any results. It
has to be the spirit of faith. It has to be spiritual. It has to be
alive. Faith has to have God operating in it. If your faith
doesn't have God working in it, then it's just a routine that
you're going through.

Whenever you add the anointing of the Spirit of God and the anointing of the Word of God into your faith, then all of a sudden your faith becomes a living force on the inside of you that God gives you to live the life He wants you to live. Now in Galatians 3, we see the importance of being a seed of Abraham. Paul's talking about Abraham and the preaching of faith and the ministry of the Word of God. He says in verse seven that only people who are of faith can be sons of Abraham. Notice that you have to get into faith to become a seed of Abraham. You can't be the seed of Abraham just because you were born in a certain country or a certain lineage or you have something natural going on. No, it's faith that gets you into the covenant of Abraham. So he says only those who are of faith are sons of Abraham.

Then in verse nine that people who are of faith are blessed with believing Abraham. Notice he says that you become a son or a daughter of Abraham by faith. How do you do that?

"And if you *are* Christ's, then you are Abraham's seed, and heirs according to the promise."
Galatians 3:29 (NKJV)

In other words, if I made Jesus Lord of my life, then I'm Abraham's seed and I'm an heir according to the promise. How do I make Jesus lord of my life? I have to do it by faith. Paul also wrote this about faith:

"For by grace you have been saved through faith, and that not of yourselves; *it is* the gift of God, not of works, lest anyone should boast." Ephesians 2:8-9 (NKJV)

Therefore, faith makes me a child of God, and it's faith that gets me in on the blessing of God. But I've only taken the first step. Now I need to learn how to operate in the blessing and receive the blessings of my walk with God in my life. How do I do it? I do it through faith. Then you drop down to verse 11 he basically says you can't become righteous. You can't enter into a righteous walk with God. Justified means righteous. In other words, I have no justification to approach the throne of God if I'm doing it on my own works. I have no right standing with God that way. So through the law, I cannot enter into a place where I'm justified in approaching God. I'm not worthy to come into His presence. I'm not able. So how do I get into the presence of God? How do I walk in righteousness? Verse 11 says the just, or the righteous, shall live by faith.

I find out here that I become a seed of Abraham through faith, operate in the blessing that God promised Abraham through faith, and then I also live by faith. So I get into the kingdom by faith, I walk in the blessings by faith, and every day I should live by faith. Faith is not something that I do when I need it. Faith is something that I do all the time. It becomes my character and becomes my nature. It becomes how I live. It becomes my attitude.

"For we walk by faith [we regulate our lives and conduct ourselves by our conviction or belief respecting man's relationship to God and divine things, with trust and holy fervor; thus we walk] not by sight *or* appearance." 2 Corinthians 5:7 (AMPC)

This is a simple Scripture in many translations, but I like this Amplified version. He is saying, "Because I walk by faith, I regulate my life and I conduct myself according to the conviction and the trust that I have in God." If I'm really living in faith, I'm always going to have an attitude of victory in my life. It doesn't mean I'm not going to have a down moment, but it means I'm not going to have a down day or a down week or a down month. When the enemy first comes in, I may get shook a little bit, but I'm a faith person. I live by faith and I've trained myself to trust in God in that situation. I've got a conviction that no matter what I find myself in, God is going to be there for me, like in Psalm 91. When you begin to look down, then David wrote that God said:

"He shall call upon Me, and I will answer him;
I *will be* with him in trouble;
I will deliver him and honor him." Psalm 91:15 (NKJV)

Therefore, I began to live with a conviction and a reliance and a trust in God. So that no matter what I'm facing, I'm not going to let what I see or *the* appearance of the problem determine my attitude. If you listen to news broadcast, they're basically all telling you bunch of junk: "The world is a mess. Everybody's a mess. Everything's a mess. We don't have a chance. This is not the country that your grandpa grew up in. Well, it is just not the same people." But I'm still breathing the same air. The generation before me, they lived in West Virginia. I still live in a state called West Virginia.

There's still things going on and bad stuff, but we can't allow the appearance that's out there to get us down. A lot of people will hear how the economy's getting worse, everything's getting worse, all this stuff's going on in the Middle East and all this stuff is going on in the Asian world and all kinds of thing. The next thing you know, they start freezing up. They're afraid to give and afraid to invest. And they're living by what they see. In that situation, you need to learn how to trust God over the situation. You need to learn how to conduct yourself and regulate your conduct based on what God is telling you to do, not what man is telling you to do. And that's the faith life. In other words, my conduct and how I approach things and how I deal with things are going to be more influenced by God than they are the world.

Then God becomes the greater influence in my life. Therefore, I'm to walk out my life in faith, being motivated by the things of God, influenced mostly by the things of God. God has say in my life so that I conduct myself as one who is trusting the Lord in whatever I'm doing. I refuse to let the world throw me into a fit of depression, throw me into a place of fear, throw me into a place where I just don't know what I'm going to do. I'm going to get up every day. I'm going to use wisdom. I'm going to pray for God to give me wisdom. But at the same time, I'm going to get up and act like Jesus is Lord. I'm going to act like He's still watching over His Word to perform it. I'm going to act like the Lord will never leave me nor forsake me.

I can boldly say the Lord is my helper. I'm not going to fear what man is going to do to me. I'm going to get up every day and trust that my God is going to make me more than a conqueror. And no matter what comes my way, greater is He that's in me than he that's against me (1 John 4:4).

> "Yet in all these things we are more than conquerors
> through Him who loved us."
> Romans 8:37 (NKJV)

I might have to fight a little harder to get it, but praise God, I'm going to get it. Because I've chosen to live a Christian life, not a fear life. I've chosen to live a Christian life, not a religious life. Religion will do alright until the pressure comes in, then religion will jump up and run. It will leave you to stand there by yourself because there's no substance to religion. But being a Christlike person, being the seed of God, knowing who you are, knowing that you're the seed of Abraham, knowing that you can walk in the blessing of Abraham, and knowing that God wants to take care of you and you're to live this thing out and walk this thing out and trust God—now you've got a strength on the inside of you that the enemy can't stop.

I want you to see another aspect of this walk of faith in Romans 8, because I've told you there's two very vital things that you're going to have to get a hold of if you're going to be able to use your faith and walk in victory. Number one, you have to know that faith begins where the will of God is known.

You can't have faith for what you don't know. Faith begins where the revelation of God's will comes in. How do you know what God's will is? It is written in the Bible.

"So then faith *comes* by hearing, and hearing by the word of God." Romans 10:17 (NKJV)

"The entrance of Your words gives light;
It gives understanding to the simple." Psalm 119:130 (NKJV)

So God enlightens us and God instructs us and lets us know what His will is based on His Word. So I have to get in the Bible and find out what God's will is. I never had faith for healing until I got a hold of the revelation from 1 Peter 2:24

and Matthew 8:17 about sickness and healing. Then I got a hold of where it all starts in Isaiah 53:4-5:

"Surely He has borne our griefs
And carried our sorrows;
Yet we esteemed Him stricken,
Smitten by God, and afflicted.
But He *was* wounded for our transgressions,
He was bruised for our iniquities;
The chastisement for our peace *was* upon Him,
And by His stripes we are healed." (NKJV)

I found out I could be healed and delivered and walk in peace and salvation.

I didn't find out that I could prosper until the revelation knowledge of God's Word came in.

"For you know the grace of our Lord Jesus Christ, that though He was rich, yet for your sakes He became poor, so that you through His poverty might become rich." 2 Corinthians 8:9 (NKJV)

I'll tell you that was a great day in my life when I got the revelation that I didn't have to stay poor the rest of my life. I didn't have to stay beat down. I didn't have to stay on the losing end all the time; I found out that I could actually prosper and God would bless me. I was so excited about it. But I didn't have a clue how to make it happen. I had God's will that He wanted me to prosper but I was so poor I couldn't pay attention.

So you not only have to find out what God's will is, you have to find the way God wants to work it in your life. The two key elements of faith are getting a hold of the revelation of God's will, the knowledge of His will, and then getting the revelation of how God wants to work His will in your life. How He wants to bring that to pass. The word way in Psalm 25 in the Hebrew means a course or mode of action. Not only do I have to find out what God wants to do for me, I need to find the course or the mode of action that God wants me to take to make that happen in my life. Now back to Romans 8.

"For as many as are led by the Spirit of God, these are sons of God." Romans 8:14 (NKJV)

You might think, "Wait. I thought God said over in Galatians 3 that the sons of God were supposed to live by faith." And then you might remember that in 2 Corinthians he said that we walk by faith and not by sight. So he says here that we're to walk by faith, but where he says we're to be led by the Spirit. So the Spirit of God must have a part to play in my faith life. You cannot have faith for something God hasn't told you to do. And your faith can never supersede the leading of the Spirit of God. You cannot override the leading of the Spirit of God by your confession. In other words, if God tells you to do it one way and you choose to do it another way, your faith will fail.

I've known ministers who were godly men. They believed
God, and God promoted them. They were blessed. They
were a great blessing to the body of Christ. And they flew
around in their own airplane and they flew in different places.
Several of them I know of were killed in airplane crashes. You
might not believe that would happen. But I can name off two
or three of them that I know personally were told by the
airport not to try to land because the weather was too bad.
But you know what happens when the Spirit of God starts
telling you don't do something, but you say, "Go ahead,
because I'm going to pray and believe God." It won't work.
Your faith will not work in that situation. You're setting
yourself up to get killed. If you're going to walk with God,
He's going to have some say on how you operate and you
cannot override what God's telling you to do. If God tells you
to stand still and you move ahead and get hit by a truck, it's
your fault. He said He wanted you to stop for a reason.

I can remember an incident years ago when I first started the
in pastoral ministry. I was driving into Charleston to meet
some ministers. It was early morning, and I was driving down
the two-lane road. I was just buzzing along, no traffic on my
side. Everything was going the other way. I came along and
about that time, something on the inside of me said, "Slow
down, slow down, slow down." I mean it just grabbed a hold
of me and said to slow down. I just thought, "What is going
on?" I felt my spirit slow down. I just hit the brakes and
started slowing down, and I didn't go another hundred feet.
There was a school bus, and a car was coming out of another

place. It pulled right out in front of me, didn't even look to see. I'd never have seen him if I'd have been going as fast as I was before I got that unction in my spirit. I would have t-boned it right in the passenger side.

If I'd thought, "I believe God will keep me safe," and kept going at speed, I would have gotten in a wreck. It would've been my fault if I got in a car wreck after the Spirit of God was trying to tell me to slow down. Thank God I was smart enough to listen to Him. You can't make your faith work when God's telling you to do something else. If God is telling you to do a certain thing a certain way, then that's how your faith works. That's the spirit of faith operating on inside of you.

So in Romans 8, Paul goes on to say:

"For you did not receive the spirit of bondage again to fear, but you received the Spirit of adoption by whom we cry out, 'Abba, Father.'" Romans 8:15 (NKJV)

It was important that Paul put verse 15 in there. He wants you to know that you can trust God. When God begins to lead you in something, you don't have to be afraid that it is not going to work. God is a good God. He sent the Spirit of adoption. We cry out, "Abba, Father." He didn't send the spirit of fear. He didn't send the spirit of bondage. He told us that we need to trust Him. In other words, God loves you and He's not going to lead you to do something that's going to be bad for you.

I'll just use giving, for instance, because you learn prosperity. I found out that I had to also be a giver and I had to sow the seed; whatever God told me to give. And I can remember the first time when we were going to school, and I was learning all this stuff. We had very little money. We just didn't have hardly any at all. One day, I actually had about $20 in my pocket and we were praising God. This is why you walk by faith and not by sight. I looked over during the praise and worship session in the school. All of the student body's in one auditorium. I looked over and the Spirit of God said, "I want you to give your $20 to that fellow." The one He pointed out had on a suit and tie. I had on a shirt and slacks. I think I had one jacket to my name a couple of ties and a couple shirts.

And I looked at him—you know, we walk by faith, not by sight—but I looked at his appearance and I thought, "Well, Lord, he looks like he's a whole lot better off than I am. He's got nicer clothes than I've got, and he's smiling and praising God. It doesn't seem like anything's wrong." And I sat there and the voice of doubt comes in as you debate with God. I talked myself right out of giving him some cash. And so I went home. God didn't come down and smack me across the mouth. I didn't think anything about it, but three days later, we were in class and they gave an opportunity to share.

The same fellow went forward. He said, "I just want to say how much I appreciate the Rhema students here and all those that are in here. And how God's helping us grow together." He said that on the same day I'd seen him that his car was sitting on empty and they didn't have any food in the house. God told him to just praise Him and He'd take care of him. So he praised God, then got in his car and got about halfway home and ran out of gas. So he was sitting out on the interstate. He said, "A student came by, saw me, recognized me, then got me some gas and gave me twenty bucks. And we got some cash for some food."

God didn't have to smack me. I smacked myself. I missed God. God was trying to bless me. Thank God, God is a good God. And He'll put up with a little bit and He won't hold grudges, but He'll give you another chance. It was about a month later, and I came walking in. Once again, I didn't have much money. We didn't have a whole lot of cash going there. I believed in God and was just learning how to prosper. I walked into the auditorium and somebody walked up and handed me a $20 bill. I knew what I could use that for and stuck it in my pocket. I got ten steps. A friend came over and said, "Hey man, you got twenty bucks?" I said, "Why?"

He said one of the students was down to the last day. If we didn't get her some money, she couldn't pay her tuition and she was going to have to step out of school. He said they needed twenty more dollars. I said, "Yeah, I got twenty dollars." God said, "The reason I gave you that twenty was not for you, but so you could be a blessing and give it to someone else." You know, whenever I learned to trust God like that and learned that I didn't have to be afraid because I had the spirit of adoption and learned that God would lead me, you know what happened? God blessed me with a better job in the afternoons and he gave Bonnie a raise. We started seeing God bless us.

To walk in faith, you also have to be led by the Spirit. You don't have to be afraid of God when He leads you. He's not going to lead you into something bad for you. He's going to lead you into something that's going to be good for you. Here's how God leads us:

"The Spirit Himself bears witness with our spirit that we are children of God." Romans 8:16 (NKJV)

You could say it like this: The Holy Spirit gives you an intuition. He gives you an unction. We can see more about the witness of the Spirit in 1 John2:20.

"But you have an anointing from the Holy One, and you know all things." 1 John 2:20 (NKJV)

"But you have been anointed by [you hold a sacred appointment from, you have been given an unction from] the Holy One, and you all know [the Truth] *or you know all things.*" 1 John 2:20 (AMPC)

You might think, "What do you mean?" The King James Version says you've been given an unction from the Holy One. That unction is the witness of God. That unction is a little push on the inside of you.

That unction is when you get ready to do something and, all of a sudden, a little check comes up in your spirit. That check is God saying, "No, don't do that." Or somebody asks you to go do something and you get that good feeling down on the inside of you, down in your spirit that it's okay. This is the thing you need to understand: When you and I are following God, God doesn't condemn us. The Holy Spirit doesn't condemn us. The Holy Spirit leads us.

> "And by this we know that we are of the truth, and shall assure our hearts before Him. For if our heart condemns us, God is greater than our heart, and knows all things."
> 1 John 3:19-20 (NKJV)

In other words, here's how I know my heart is right. If my heart condemns me, God is greater than my heart and knows all things, beloved. If our heart does not condemn us, we have confidence toward God. The Holy Spirit doesn't condemn anybody; your own heart condemns you. The Holy Spirit witnesses to you. The Holy Spirit gives you either a green light or a check. And John said that the Spirit bears witness with your spirit. It's not in your head that you get this. It's not in your feelings of your body that you get this, but it's down inside, down in your inner man. Have you ever done anything and while you're doing it, you just felt sick to your stomach? That's the Holy Ghost trying to tell you to stop.

The worst deal I ever made in my life was for a car. I really liked this car and they had everything on it I wanted. It was the right color, it was everything I wanted, but it was too expensive. I've learned a little bit since then. But I wanted this car, and I went down and this guy finally came out. He told me what the final deal was and how much the monthly payment was. Down on the inside of me, I was thinking, "Get up, run. Don't look back. Don't even let them know what your name is. Just get up and run real quick; get out of here. Flee the very appearance of evil. And this is evil—run."

But instead of listening to that unction or that witness down inside of me and that gut feeling, if you just want to say it that way, but that check that God was giving me, I thought, "Well, I'll tell you what I'll do. I'll put this off on Bonnie. I'll call her and tell her how much the monthly payment is. And she'll say, 'Honey, you know we can't afford that.' And then I'll say, 'Well, my wife's not agreement. So we can't do it.'" I was just going to throw her under the bus. It'd be my wife's fault that we didn't buy the car. I called Bonnie up and I said, "Now, honey, here's what it is. And here's how much the monthly payment is." I was waiting on her to tell me no. She said, "Well, honey, if you like the car, whatever you think." I just believe God, you hear from God. Bye and hangs up on me. She threw me under the bus. Amen. I went against the unction of my spirit and signed the paper, drove the car home, and enjoyed it for thirty days.

Then the first payment came due, and I stopped enjoying the car. I tried to sell that car. But the moment I drove it off the parking lot, I owed more than it was worth. I tried to get somebody else to trade me, and they wouldn't give me enough. I ended up driving that car and ended up paying it all off. God said, "You're going to learn a lesson here. I'll supply the need, but you're going to have to believe me with everything in you and every month to get it." It was a struggle, but we got there. We drove that car for about seven years and put over hundred thousand miles plus on it. Then we sowed that car into a family as a seed. It was still a pretty good car because I take care of them. The devil may have got me in the beginning, but I got blessed in the end. But I made the decision that I am never going to sign anything whenever I'm getting that check on the inside of me saying, "Don't do it." Faith will not work against the check or the unction of the anointing of God on the inside of you.

When we bought another car, I learned this time. When I went in, I just looked at the contract and I said to the sales person, "This is just too much. I can't do it. And I'd regret it. I've made this mistake before. God bless you. Thank you for helping me." He looked at me. "Can we do anything?" I said no, he couldn't change what was going on in my spirit, so he couldn't change anything out here. I left, but a week later, I was driving by and saw this car that was better than the one that I wanted. I walked in, and it was half the price. The guy gave me a better deal and we could afford it. God blessed me greatly because I listened to him.

There are two ways to learn. You can mess it up yourself or you can listen to somebody else's mess up. John says you have an unction from the Holy One. When you're making decisions in faith, you need to pray and listen to what the Spirit of God is saying. Is God telling you to do that? If God's not telling you to do that, it is not going to work. I don't care how good it looks. You need to listen to the Spirit. The Spirit of God is trustworthy. The Holy Ghost will guide you in the way you're supposed to go. That unction is the witness of the Spirit: Is God telling you yes or is God telling you no. God telling you to sit on it or is God telling you to run ahead.

As you learn to listen to the unction and you get comfortable with that, all of a sudden you begin to learn how to walk by faith. You get to learn how to operate in the spirit of faith. You begin to learn how to let God help you make decisions in every area of life. Whenever you have heard from God, and you've got that release in your spirit and your heart is giving you yes and amen, then you know your faith can work at its maximum because you're in God's perfect will. We need to learn these things.

You've also got to remember, John said the Spirit bears witness with our spirit. So you need to know what your spirit is. I told you the spirit is your heart. Let's look at it in Romans 2 as well.

> "For he is not a Jew who *is one* outwardly, nor *is* circumcision that which *is* outward in the flesh; but *he is* a Jew who *is one* inwardly; and circumcision *is that* of the heart, in the Spirit, not in the letter; whose praise *is* not from men but from God." Romans 2:28-29 (NKJV)

Just because you went through the ritual of outward circumcision, it doesn't make you a Jew in the eyes of God anymore. So what is it that God's looking for? Paul says this, but he is a Jew who is one inwardly and has had circumcision that is of the heart. He's not talking about your physical organ, that pumps blood throughout your veins. You cut on it, you're in trouble. He goes on to link the heart to the spirit. So your heart is your spirit. When the Word says that the Spirit of God bears witness with your spirit, it's saying the Spirit of God bears witness with your heart. It's your heart. You've got to learn to follow.

Have you found that when you get into a situation, your greatest battle is between your head and your heart? If your head's telling you one thing, your heart is telling you another, you better follow your heart because your heart is where God's trying to show you what to do. It's in your heart that the Holy Spirit is witnessing to you. Can you trust the Holy Spirit? Sure you can.

"'If you love Me, keep My commandments. And I will pray the Father, and He will give you another Helper, that He may abide with you forever—the Spirit of truth, whom the world cannot receive, because it neither sees Him nor knows Him; but you know Him, for He dwells with you and will be in you.'" John 14:15-17 (NKJV)

"'However, when He, the Spirit of truth, has come, He will guide you into all truth; for He will not speak on His own *authority,* but whatever He hears He will speak; and He will tell you things to come."
John 16:13 (NKJV)

The Holy Spirit will show you the right way to go. He'll show you the right decisions to make. You and I have to get so bold and confident in our trust of God and our faith in God that we can trust the leading of the Spirit and trust our ability to hear Him. This is the thing to remember as you train up your spirit and as you listen to that witness: sometimes you just have to take a little time and wait and pray. But all of a sudden, as you get sensitive to God down on the inside of you, you either have a green light to go ahead and do it, or you'll have a red light that says no. There'll be a check there in your spirit. But whenever you or somebody says, "Let's go do this" but down on the inside, everything goes, "Ooh. Yeah, that's good. Praise God. That's right. Let's go do that."

That's the Spirit of God bearing witness in your spirit, showing you that it's okay, showing you that this is what God wants you to do. The Spirit of God, at times will talk to you. But a lot of times, He just gives you an unction. He just gives you a nudge to go a certain direction.

I shared about my shoulder. I prayed and prayed and prayed. Finally, the Lord said, "Go have it checked out." I felt that in my spirit. I'm having tremendous success because I found out how the Holy Spirit was leading me to do it this time. At the same time, the Lord spoke to me as I was praying, and He didn't just come down and stand in my office and talk to me. But in my spirit, I sensed, I was supposed to sow a seed and do certain things. And I said, "I'll do that." But it kind of got away from me. I was praying a little later on and the Lord said, "When are you going to do what I told you to do?" I did it that day because I know that when the Spirit of God is bearing witness or leading me to do something, there's a blessing attached to it. But I have to obey that and use my faith and act on what He's telling me to do to release that blessing back into my life.

Faith has to have the Word of God in operation, but faith also has to have the leading of the Holy Spirit in operation inside of us. Let's look again at Romans:

> "For I delight in the law of God according to the
> inward man." Romans 7:22 (NKJV)

My inward man is the guy down on the inside of me that desires to do the things of God. It's my spirit that's going to lead me with the unction or the leading of the Holy Spirit. As I trust God and walk with God my spirit will delight in doing what God's told me to do.

What's funny is you don't ever judge whether you did the right thing with God by how you feel in your mental realm. For instance, I've been sitting there and Spirit of God leads me in giving. I feel like a certain amount I'm supposed to give. It was stretching my faith a little bit, and I pray about it. I keep getting that unction: "I should do this. I should do this. I should do this." So I go ahead and write it out, and Bonnie and I pray over it. And we agree, and when you do it, you're just delighting in the Word and your inward man. But ten minutes later, after they've taken it up, your head goes, "Boy, you stupid thing. What are you going to do now? Man, you're a fool. Why would you do that?"

All of a sudden, you just feel like, "Oh God, what am I going to do now?" Because the thief comes immediately to steal the Word and steal the blessing. You need to cast that down. You say, "Glory to God. I just put seed out into the kingdom of

God. And I put it in the hands of the Lord. I'll tell you what I'm going to do now, devil: I'm going to watch God multiply my seed and bless me. I just obeyed what the Holy Ghost was telling me to do. And I did it in faith." You learn these things, but you have to learn to follow the leading of the Holy Spirit.

Sometimes we're looking for something spectacular. We want the minister to come out and call us out and prophesy over us and tell us all these wonderful things. That may happen and it may not. They did it in the book of Acts. Do you know the book of Acts spans little more than thirty years? In those thirty years, some of the great apostles only had two visions. In that thirty year span, they only did a few spectacular things. Most of the time, it was ministry of the Word, helping people live for God and healings and things like that. We read the book of Acts, and we think it happened in thirty minutes or thirty days. The spectacular happens as God leads, but the supernatural is operating all the time. And the witness of the Spirit is just as supernatural as the spectacular. So don't miss out on what God wants to do by looking for something spectacular, like an angel showing up or a word of prophecy.

Learn to listen to what the Spirit of God is saying to you. Before you step out in faith, just stop and say, "Lord, you know what I need to do. And I've got the Holy Spirit living in me. Holy Spirit, I'm asking you to bear witness in my spirit and show me what I need to do." Then let the Spirit of God witness to you and let Him show you what to do and follow the leading of the Holy Ghost. That's when your faith works. When the enemy comes up and tries to stop you, you can say, "Wait a minute. I want you to know I'm doing this based on the Scripture in the Bible." And you speak the Word to him. And then you say, "The reason I'm doing this is because I have a clear witness in my spirit that God wants me to do it. And I'm going to follow the leading of the Holy Ghost. Now I'm going to do what God tells me to do."

I heard Pastor Hagin tell a story of when he was a young teenager. He was with his buddies and they were riding around and doing some things on a Friday night. They decided to go over to this other town. They got about five miles outside of town. One of them said, "Yeah, we'll go down here and do this, this and this." And he said, "No, wait a minute. We can't do it." When they insisted, he told them to stop the car. They said, "What do you mean stop?" He said, "Stop the car. I'm not going on. I don't care what you call me. I'm not doing it. Stop the car." So they stopped the car.

He got out and he told them he had a bad feeling about this. He was getting a witness in his spirit that they ought not do it. He told them not go there and to leave it alone. "Oh, you're just chicken," they said. They took off in the car. He turned and walked five miles back into town. He said the next morning he found out that they went over and got in trouble. All four of them got arrested and put in jail. Their dads had to go over to the other town and bail them out. He was so glad the preacher's kid listened to the Holy Ghost.

How many times have we just gone against that unction and somebody else got us in trouble? We need to learn, especially in the hour we're living in, God will protect us. God will guide us. God will show us when not to act and when to act, but you have to use your faith and be bold. You have to step out and say, "Nope, I'm not going against the unction of the Spirit. I'm not going against the leading of the Holy Ghost because the Holy Ghost is a genius. If I listen to Him, He'll make me look smart too. He knows what's coming, and He knows how to protect me and keep me from being a part of the problem and help me to be a part of the answer."

God will walk with us. He'll show us, He'll guide us. The first way He's going to do it is He's going to witness to our spirit. Just a simple yes or a simple no; a simple check if not right or simple green light of yes and amen, go do it. When you get that velvety smooth yes, you get freedom in your spirit. Then we have assurance that we've heard from God. When we do that, we're going to walk in victory. That's how you make your faith work in every situation.

CHAPTER THREE

As we begin this chapter, I want to look at some powerful truths the Lord Jesus taught in John 10. Before we look at these truths, it would do us well to look again at some of Paul's words to the Corinthians.

> "And since we have the same spirit of faith, according to what is written, 'I believed and therefore I spoke,' we also believe and therefore speak." 2 Corinthians 4:13 (NKJV)

It's the spirit of faith. We have to have the spirit of faith. Faith cannot be just a legalistic thing in your life. You cannot get results from God just because you follow the steps. If you're going to get results from God, you have to have a living faith. It's got to be the spirit of faith, not the letter, the letter kills but the Spirit gives life. This has to become real to you. It's must become a lifestyle.

> "But that no one is justified by the law in the sight of God *is* evident, for 'the just shall live by faith.'"
> Galatians 3:11 (NKJV)

Those who have been justified, made righteous by the blood of Jesus Christ, we're to live our lives in faith. What is faith?

Faith is trusting in God. Faith is having assurance in God. Faith is having such a conviction that God will do for you what He said He would do that you step out and believe it. In fact, you not only step out and believe it, you start talking about it. When we look at God's Word, He says that faith has two elements operating. It is the spirit of faith, which means it has to operate by the help of the Holy Spirit on the inside of you. Then it says, according to that which is written, we believed; in other words, my believing is based upon what God says in His Word. That believing comes alive by the Spirit of God working in my life.

So it is the Word and the Spirit operating in me that causes my faith to be a living force on the inside of me. It's what separates me and distinguishes me from somebody who doesn't have a relationship with God. I get so into trusting God that my faith becomes such a living part of my life that it becomes my attitude. It becomes the way I conduct myself. It becomes my opinion; it becomes my lifestyle. I begin to live this way and I live with an expectancy in me. I believe that God is, and that He's going to reward me (see Hebrews 11:6). I believe that He's going to take care of me and He's going to do what His Word says. It brings such a conviction in my life that as Paul said we also believe and therefore speak. In other words, I believe it so much, have such a conviction, and it's such a living thing in me that I'm willing to talk about it. I'm not afraid to say that I trust in God. I'm not afraid to say that I believe God's going to get me through because I'm living in my faith with God. I'm living in my trust with God and the conviction that God will do it is greater than the fear that He won't.

I begin to trust God with a simple trust in my heart. Kind of like if you tell your child, "We will do this." We've got two granddaughters, and with both of them it has pretty much been the same that when I told them I would get them something, they believed it. Ava's older now, but when Carly was about to turn three I told her over the phone, as we were doing FaceTime with her mom, that Papaw was going to get her a present. Carly just stopped, looked at her mom and said, "Mama, Papaw's getting me a present. She just throws the phone down and goes running through the house because she trusts in my words. In other words: he said it, that settles it. I'm going to get it now. She starts talking and singing little songs about what I'm getting her. I'm here, she's there. I haven't done anything yet, but she's going on my word. She trusts what I said to her. Jesus said unless we enter in like a little child, we can't really experience it the way He wants us to (see Matthew 18). In other words, when God speaks to us and God begins to lead us, we have to have that childlike faith to the point where we just begin to get excited. Because God said it, we believe it and we're going to act like He's going to do it. As you press in and you learn how to be led by the Spirit and learn how to trust God through His Word, that's the type of faith that He wants to bring you into. We can grow our faith to that level of trust, that when we get into God's presence and He speaks something to us, even though we don't feel it, even though it doesn't look like it, even though everybody around us is saying it may not happen, we have a trust that goes beyond what we can see or feel because our faith is in God, in His integrity, and in His love for us that He will do what He said He would do.

I'm led by faith and I'm also led by the Spirit, as we saw in 2 Corinthians 5 and Romans 8. So faith and the Holy Ghost work hand in hand together to get me going in the direction God wants me to go. If the Holy Spirit is going to lead me, then I need to learn how to follow.

The Lord Jesus here in John 10 gives some absolute truth that we need to get a hold of if we're going to be led by the Lord, the Spirit, and the Word and learn to walk in faith and walk in a way that we trust Him no matter what we see or feel. We need to believe God's going to do for us what He said He would do. It will create such a conviction in my heart that I'm bold to stand up and speak it out.

"'Most assuredly, I say to you, he who does not enter the sheepfold by the door, but climbs up some other way, the same is a thief and a robber. But he who enters by the door is the shepherd of the sheep. To him the doorkeeper opens, and the sheep hear his voice; and he calls his own sheep by name and leads them out. And when he brings out his own sheep, he goes before them; and the sheep follow him, for they know his voice. Yet they will by no means follow a stranger, but will flee from him, for they do not know the voice of strangers.'"
John 10:1-5 (NKJV)

Jesus is talking here. He's saying whoever tries to come in and get authority without doing it the right way is a thief and a robber. He's telling us there's a possible thief and a robber who has tried to get into the sheep fold, tried to get into this world. But the true shepherd uses the door. In other words, there's a way that God wants it done and he that does it the way God wants it becomes the shepherd of the sheep. The door that Jesus is talking about here is the door of being birthed into this world through natural childbirth, through the woman. We know that Jesus came into this world being born of a woman. He said in John 5:27 that He had authority on the earth because He's the Son of Man. In other words, Jesus being born a man gave Him authority on the earth.

Satan is the thief and the robber because he came in another way. He stole his authority. He got involved with mankind because of Adam's sin. He's a thief and a robber, but Jesus came through the door, through the virgin birth, to become the shepherd of the sheep.

In verse three, we see that this shepherd speaks to us. The sheep know His voice and follow Him. In verse 5, He says they will not follow a stranger's voice. If you're going to follow the Lord, you have to know His voice. You've got to be led by Him. Faith cannot operate outside of your walk with Jesus.

Faith is so you can please God and follow after God. It's so you can do the works of Jesus Christ and have an intimate relationship with Jesus. Because God is a God of faith.

"By faith we understand that the [c]worlds were framed by the word of God, so that the things which are seen were not made of things which are visible…But without faith *it is* impossible to please *Him,* for he who comes to God must believe that He is, and *that* He is a rewarder of those who diligently seek Him." Hebrews 11:3, 6 (NKJV)

Jesus has come to give us faith. He's the one who imparts faith to us. The reason is so that we can follow Him, that we can know God, and we can live the God kind of life right here on this earth. Now following the Lord, hearing His voice and letting Him tell us what to do is to be the foundation of our walk of faith.

"'I am the door. If anyone enters by Me, he will be saved, and will go in and out and find pasture. The thief does not come except to steal, and to kill, and to destroy. I have come that they may have life, and that they may have *it* more abundantly…And other sheep I have which are not of this fold; them also I must bring, and they will hear My voice; and there will be one flock *and* one shepherd.'"
John 10:9, 10, 16 (NKJV)

Verse 16 gets me all excited. So it's not just the ones there with Him at that time, but those coming in later, we're going to be able to hear His voice, just like they could hear His voice. There's not a Jewish church and a Gentile church. There's only a church. There's only one shepherd, one Lord and one Messiah and His name is Jesus.

"'My sheep hear My voice, and I know them, and
they follow Me.'" John 10:27 (NKJV)

Notice here that the Lord is talking about Him being the good shepherd. He's talking about that He came to call His sheep out. He said there in verse 3 that He calls His sheep and leads them out. What's He leading them out of? In verse 9, He told us He's the door. Jesus is saying, "I've come to bring you out of your sin and out of bondage and out from under the control of darkness. I've come to bring you into salvation if you'll listen to my voice." You can't get saved unless you hear God's voice speaking. Jesus has to call you. He has to speak to you. He stands at the door of your heart and knocks, and you hear His voice and you open up and He comes in. The good news of the gospel is that Jesus speaks to all and calls us all out of sin into salvation.

Jesus says that as the good shepherd, He's come to lay down His life for you and He's come to speak to you. His sheep will hear His voice and He will take you and bring you out of sin. Bring you out of darkness, bring you out of the control of Satan and bring you over into salvation. He will bring you into a place where you can have life and have it more abundantly. Jesus says all of this is really going to be based on you being able to hear His voice, know His voice and follow His voice.

Let's look again at verse five. He's said we are to use our faith to follow the Lord, to do what He's telling us to do. But verse five says, yet they will not follow a stranger, but will run from him. Notice that singular noun: a stranger. He's distinguishing this as an individual, but then He says they don't know the voice of strangers, plural. The stranger is Satan and the strangers are his demon forces that go out and do his bidding. Jesus says that we're not to listen to the voice of the devil nor to the taunting lies of the demons that he sends out to come against us.

If you look the word stranger up in the Greek, it means hostile, foreign, and not akin to him. He's saying there that the stranger's voice is hostile to the things of God. That's how you know it's a stranger's voice. The stranger's voice is a foreign voice. In other words, you don't quite understand it. The stranger's voice is not akin to God's. That means it is not in relation. It has no relation to the shepherd. It is a total contrary voice that is trying to get you to do something other than what the shepherd is telling you to do.

"There are, it may be, so many kinds of languages in the
world, and none of them *is* without significance. Therefore, if
I do not know the meaning of the language, I shall be a
foreigner to him who speaks, and he who speaks *will be* a
foreigner to me." 1 Corinthians 14:10-11 (NKJV)

In other words, if I don't understand the voice, I'm just kind
of lost. I just don't know what to do. There are a lot of voices
vying for your attention. Have you ever gotten to a place
where you just said, "Lord, I just need to do this, but man, I
don't know if I need to do this or I need to do that." Have
you ever decided you're going to live for God and all of a
sudden you have all kinds of thoughts come to your head
about why you can't live for God? Maybe you've said you're
going to go up to the altar and give your heart to Jesus.
Immediately, some little voice says, "Yeah, but you got a
party planned for tomorrow night and you got this stuff that
you've bought already and you don't want to waste a good
bag of dope." There are a lot of voices, strange voices that are
hostile to you serving God. Maybe you've said, "I'm going to
fast tomorrow and pray and believe God." Then immediately
you begin to think about your trip to your favorite store, your
favorite coffee and your favorite donut and all these thoughts.
You can't go to sleep thinking about all of the things you
want to eat today and tomorrow. Nobody's ever had that
problem?

There is a stranger's voice that's hostile to you pressing in and following God. In other words, you can follow the wrong voice. In fact, the very entrance of Satan to society, the introduction of the devil to humanity, is found in Genesis 3 when he comes to Eve and questions what God had said.

> "And he said to the woman, 'Has God indeed said,
> "You shall not eat of every tree of the garden"?'
>
> And the woman said to the serpent, 'We may eat the fruit of the trees of the garden; but of the fruit of the tree which *is* in the midst of the garden, God has said, "You shall not eat it, nor shall you touch it, lest you die." ' "
>
> Then the serpent said to the woman, 'You will not surely die. For God knows that in the day you eat of it your eyes will be opened, and you will be like God, knowing good and evil.'"
> Genesis 3:1-5 (NKJV)

That serpent's voice was hostile to God. That was totally contrary to God's Word that He'd given to them. It was foreign to what God had said to them. It had nothing in relationship to God, and Adam and Eve failed. They didn't discern the voice of a stranger.

A lot of times our faith is failing us because we're not discerning the voice of the stranger. We're not discerning the right voice. We're not getting ourselves in a place where we can hear what the shepherd is telling us to do. How do you know if it's the shepherd speaking to you? He said that He would lead us into salvation and that He would bring us into life and life more abundantly. When Jesus is speaking to us, it's going to produce something good. Jesus is never going to tell you to go get drunk. He's never going to go tell you to cheat on somebody. He's never going to tell you to get mad. He's never going to tell you not to go to church, and He's never going to lead you in a way that's going to bring harm to you. It's the thief who brings harm. It's the stranger who comes to steal, kill, and destroy, and it's his words that are going to bring destruction to you. It's his words that are going to kill your faith. It's his words that are full of fear. It's his words that are telling you you're not worthy. It's his words that are telling you that you can't get it. It's his words that tell you you're not worthy to get it. It's his words that tell you you'll never be spiritual enough. It's his words that tell you that you made too many mistakes.

All these voices are going on. But when you decide you're going to do what God tells you and use your faith, I'll guarantee you there'll be all kinds of thoughts and all kinds of words and all kinds of voices hitting your head. They'll tell you that you can't measure up and you'll never get it. When you're standing and believing God for something and every time you turn around, you're hearing something saying it ain't going to happen and you should just give up, that's the stranger's voice. That's the enemy trying to stop you from walking this thing out in faith and trusting God. You might wonder how you know the Lord's voice and how does He speak to you?

Remember in John 14, Jesus said:

> "'If you love Me, keep My commandments. And I will pray
> the Father, and He will give you another Helper, that He may
> abide with you forever." (v 15-16 NKJV)

That word "helper" is paraclete, meaning, one called alongside, one like me. One scholar said one just like me, one to take my place. In other words, the Holy Spirit is going to come, and He's going to be called alongside us as our helper. He's just like Jesus. In fact, He is here as Jesus' representative.

He also said in that chapter that if we do the Word of God and abide in him, then the Father and the Son would come and make their home in us (v 23). They can make their home in us by the Holy Spirit dwelling on the inside of us. As we read in Luke 24, Jesus has a flesh and bone body that's seated on the right hand of the throne of God. Right now, Jesus has a physical body. It's glorified, it's covered in light, He has His own body. Jesus physically cannot come and live in you. Jesus physically is not on the earth right now. Other than working through you and me, the person Jesus Christ is seated at the right hand of God on the throne of God in heaven, waiting until His enemies are made His footstool.

On the day of Pentecost, He sent the Holy Spirit and the Holy Spirit came to bring His anointing, His life and all that He did into our lives and Jesus lives in us now by the power of the Holy Spirit and the Holy Spirit unites us to Jesus and we become one spirit with the Lord.

When you get to heaven, you're going to look around and you're going to have a glorified body. You're going to see Jesus Christ, the son of God, in His glorified body on the throne of God. We're all going to bow before Him. He's not going to be in us. He's going to be standing right there before us. Brother Hagin has shared visions about seeing the Lord. The first time, he said he just fell at His feet and began to say, "Lord, I'm so unworthy." And the Lord reached down and lifted him up and said, "No, you are worthy because I made you worthy. Now stand strong." And he said he stood there standing and trembling. One other time he was meditating in the afternoon. He was actually in his bed and the door opened up and Jesus came walking in. Brother Hagin said He's about five foot ten and about 185 pounds. He said He had on a robe and Roman sandals that time. He came over, pulled up a chair, and sat down. That was discerning of spirits. Now Jesus was seated at the throne of God, but He came down through the Spirit, and He walked into that place in a vision and spoke to Brother Hagin. Jesus has appeared to others throughout the Bible.

Jesus is the shepherd. He's Lord God Almighty and we are created in His image. Maybe not outwardly yet, but inwardly, we've become a new creation in Christ Jesus. Old things are passed away. All things become new, and we are formed as Him (see 2 Corinthians 5:17). In our inward man, we look like Jesus. That means we are looking good.

I hope you begin to understand what He's trying to speak to us in John 16. He sent the Holy Spirit to dwell in us as our helper and guide.

"'I still have many things to say to you, but you cannot bear *them* now. However, when He, the Spirit of truth, has come, He will guide you into all truth; for He will not speak on His own *authority,* but whatever He hears He will speak; and He will tell you things to come.'" John 16:12-13 (NKJV)

Jesus wanted to show us even more, He said, as the Great Shepherd, He would speak to us through the Holy Spirit. The Holy Spirit relays to us what He hears Jesus say on the throne. I don't care how many millions and billions there are on the earth. If we all got saved at once and called out to Jesus, He's great enough to speak individually to each one of us. And the Holy Ghost can relay to each one of us a personal message from God twenty-four/seven for the rest of our lives and never get overwhelmed. Heaven never finds itself running out of power. The Holy Spirit guides us. The Holy Spirit has come to show us what Jesus wants us to do. The Holy Spirit has come to be the voice of Jesus speaking into our lives. So the Holy Spirit doesn't represent Himself. The Holy Spirit represents Jesus to us, and He comes and lives on the inside of us because He is a spirit.

He comes and lives in my spirit, and I become filled with the Spirit and the anointing of the Holy Ghost is in me. The Holy Spirit begins to speak in my spirit. Some people say, "Well, I thought the Holy Spirit spoke in tongues." No, as Acts 2:4 says:

"And they were all filled with the Holy Spirit and began to speak with other tongues, as the Spirit gave them utterance." (NKJV)

Paul said:

"For if I pray in a tongue, my spirit prays, but my understanding is unfruitful." 1 Corinthians 14:14 (NKJV)

In other words, when tongues are used, my head checks out. My spirit man takes over. The Holy Spirit doesn't speak in tongues, if He did we wouldn't know what He was saying. He speaks to us in our language. You know how much of a genius He is? If you speak Spanish, the Holy Spirit talks to you in Spanish. If you speak German, the Holy Spirit speaks to you in German.

He's relaying to you what your Shepherd is trying to tell you so that you can use your faith and follow Him out of your problem and over into the victory that He's already purchased for you. Your faith will not work without you hearing the voice of God. You have to know what the Lord wants you to do before your faith can really work for you. You have to know it's God's will and have a 100 percent conviction that you can have it. Just a little bit of doubt and unbelief can hinder you from having enough conviction to be bold enough, to follow the Lord right through the battle. Sometimes you have to follow the Good Shepherd right through the fire. You have to get out and walk on some water with Him every now and then. You have to walk through the flood with Him sometimes.

"When you pass through the waters, I *will be* with you;
And through the rivers, they shall not overflow you.
When you walk through the fire, you shall not be burned,
Nor shall the flame scorch you." Isaiah 43:2 (NKJV)

Sometimes for you to get from where you're at to where God wants you to be, you have to get in behind your Good Shepherd and trust the Holy Spirit to guide you into the truth and speak to you and show you how to use your faith and walk right through that thing. But if you're convinced in your heart that God has showed you, I don't care how hot it is. You can be like the three Hebrew children. You can have a party in the furnace (see Daniel 3).

People will look at you and they say, "How can you be so calm?" You can say, "My shepherd has gone before me. He said He would go before me and lead me." Jesus doesn't tell you to do something and leave you alone. He said His sheep follow Him. That means I can go through that fire because I know my Lord and my Shepherd has already gone before me. He's going to show me exactly how to get through this mess until I get to the other side. Jesus knows every rock I need to step on. He knows where all the mine traps are, and He knows how to get me through to the other side. So I have to learn to listen to Him and trust Him to guide me through. That's why you have to hear the voice of God.

"For as many as are led by the Spirit of God, these are sons of God." Romans 8:14 (NKJV)

As a son of God, I'm to be led by the Spirit of God. In light of what Jesus said in John 10 and what He also said again in John 16, to be led by the Spirit of God is to be led by the Good Shepherd because the Holy Spirit is not operating on His authority. He's not operating independently. The Holy Spirit is only doing what Jesus tells Him to do. Therefore I could say it like this: for as many as are led by the Lord Jesus, the Good Shepherd, these are the sons of God because Jesus leads us by the power of the Holy Spirit. The Holy Spirit speaks to us what He hears the Father and the Son talking about on the throne. He guides us into all truth and shows us the right way to go.

For you did not receive the spirit of bondage again to fear (see Romans 8), so that should let you know a little bit about the Holy Spirit. If you're afraid, then it's probably not God. Somebody says, "How do I know the Lord is leading me in this." What is it producing? Fear, worry, anxiety, skepticism, anxiousness, fretting? That's probably not the voice of the Lord. That's probably not the Good Shepherd. Every time Jesus showed up, He'd say, "Be not afraid" and "Don't fear." In other words, the first thing Jesus does is get you over into peace with Him. You've not received the spirit of bondage. If it's leading into bondage, it is probably not the Holy Ghost because we haven't received the spirit of bondage. Therefore, if you feel bound, then it's probably not God. Jesus came to set us free.

> "Now the Lord is the Spirit; and where the Spirit of the
> Lord *is*, there *is* liberty."
> 2 Corinthians 3:17 (NKJV)

That means where the Holy Spirit is, there's liberty, emancipation from bondage, and freedom. Paul says in Romans 8 that you receive the spirit of adoption that lets us cry out, "Abba, Father." Notice that when the Holy Ghost gets involved in your life, He'll get involved in your mouth. You can't follow God without talking. Even when you get saved, you have to declare Jesus as Lord to get saved. Then if you get filled with the Holy Ghost and the Spirit of God's leading, you have the same spirit of faith. We believe according to what God said in His Word, and we believe so much, we spoke. Your tongue, James says in James 3, is like a rudder of a ship. James says if you don't learn how to let your tongue direct your ship, all the winds of the sea are going to toss you every which way and you're never going to get anything. But if you let God get control of your tongue, then your tongue can maneuver you and guide you from one place to another. I don't care how bad the wind is. I don't care how tough those waves are. You can talk yourself right through that thing with the help of the Holy Ghost.

Now this is what else He says, the Spirit Himself (Romans 8:16). I mean, God is involved with me in this thing. God Himself is walking me through this. Glory to God. Somebody says, how can you be so confident? God's with me. Lord, do we go through door one, door two, door three, whichever you go through, I'm going through.

I took a couple of ministers on a ministry trip I was doing back in the nineties. The missionary I work with had a mission house and there was a pastor who lived there. It was his home and he was a great man of God. If we would happen to go out anywhere and eat, I said, "Let me give you a little advice: order whatever they order because it will be safe. They won't order anything that wouldn't be good. They know the place."

We'd been there for a week and we were heading to the airport to go back home. I said, "Well, let's get something to eat before we go there." We were flying on some little plane. It was not going to have anything to eat. So we stopped into this place and my missionary friend said this place had good little personal pizzas and Coke. We asked, "Is it still good, though?" The local pastor we worked with said it was good and we should go.

We went in, and you could get a cheese pizza and ice-cold Coca-Cola. So my missionary friend orders pizza and Coca-Cola. The pastor orders cheese pizza and Coca-Cola. I ordered pizza and Coca-Cola. The other friends said, "I want this chicken and this and this." I thought they were nuts. I tried to warn them. Then the server brought my missionary friend his pizza, the pastor's pizza, and my pizza, and our ice-cold Coca-Colas. Then they brought out the mystery food. You couldn't tell what it was. They looked at that and picked around it. I said, "You eat every bit of it. You were dumb enough to order it. I told you not to go off on your own." So the three of us sat there and enjoyed our cheese pizzas and we wouldn't even give the others a bite.

I bring up that story because it's like the Lord saying, "Let's go through door one." But you say, "I'm going to try three." God knows someone's standing over behind door three with a hammer and you're going to get hit right between the eyes when you walk through it. The Lord knows which door you should walk through. The Lord Himself bears witness with

DISCOVERING GOD'S WILL AND WAY

our spirit that we are children of God. In other words, the Holy Ghost wants to show you. He wants to bear witness. He wants to be involved in your decision making. It's the Spirit of God. He will bear witness with me and He will bear witness with my spirit. The Holy Spirit always leads me in my spirit. Jesus always talks to me in my heart, not my head. My head may be saying, "Don't do it." My flesh may be saying, "I can't do it." But in my heart, there's a witness down there that says I can get to where God said I can go. It will work for me and the Holy Spirit's right there to walk me through this thing to get me to the other side.

You still might wonder how you can know if it's the Holy Spirit. I can give you a couple of answers.

> "For there are three that bear witness in heaven: the Father, the Word, and the Holy Spirit; and these three are one." 1 John 5:7 (NKJV)

Now we know that Jesus is the Word from John 1. Therefore the Word of God, both the living Word and the written Word, will always be in agreement with the Spirit of God. The Holy Ghost will never lead you contrary to the Word of God. One time I had a man tell me the Spirit of God was leading him to divorce his wife and marry another man's wife. He said, "Yeah, I prayed about it and the Spirit bore witness with me, and she believes it. So we both believe it's God that we divorce and then I can remarry."

I said, "Find me one Scripture in the whole Bible to back this up. I'll do you one better: find me half of a Scripture in the Bible that tells you to do that. No, I'll do you one better than that: Find me half a Scripture out of context in the Bible that can tell you that you're supposed to do that then I'll believe that was the Holy Ghost." That wasn't the voice of his Lord and shepherd. That was the voice of a stranger, trying to wreck their lives, wreck their home, wreck everything about them. I said, "Now cast that stupid spirit out of you and get yourself back in love with your wife and back in love with your husband and let the Holy Ghost help you through this thing. I don't want to hear that anymore."

People say all kinds of things they say came from the Spirit. "The Holy Ghost told me, you know, I'm not supposed to tithe." Or "The Lord told me I'm not supposed to have those things operate in my life." I said, "Well, then God's a respecter of persons because they're operating in my life." Are you telling me, "God loves me more than He loves you." I said, "No He doesn't, you just need to bring your flesh into submission to God, get into the Bible and submit to God's Word."

The Spirit of God will help you, and yet He'll always speak the truth of God's Word, as John 16:13 and John 17:17 say. That means the Holy Spirit is the spirit of the Word. He brings the truth of the Word to you and shows you how to apply it in your life.

"Who *is* wise and understanding among you? Let him show by good conduct *that* his works *are done* in the meekness of wisdom. But if you have bitter envy and self-seeking in your hearts, do not boast and lie against the truth. This wisdom does not descend from above, but *is* earthly, sensual, demonic. For where envy and self-seeking *exist,* confusion and every evil thing *are* there. But the wisdom that is from above is first pure, then peaceable, gentle, willing to yield, full of mercy and good fruits, without partiality and without hypocrisy. Now the fruit of righteousness is sown in peace by those who make peace." James 3:13-18 (NKJV)

James says to have the wise person demonstrate his wisdom, let him live it out. Wisdom is the ability to do what you know; wisdom is the ability to use knowledge. Knowledge is one thing, but wisdom is how to apply that knowledge. So he's saying that wisdom is God leading you on how to use your faith and get done what you need to do. He goes on to warn against lying against the Word. In other words, if you're going against the Word, don't say God told you to do it. James says this kind of wisdom is selfish. It's sensual. It's your flesh telling you. He says that it's demonic. The stranger's voice is talking to you, and he's making you self-seeking. He's making you envious. He's making you jealous. You're doing it out of insecurity. You're doing it for what's in it for you, not concerned about anybody else. He said that's the wrong voice. That's not God.

If you want to know how God operates, let's look at verse 17. The King James Version says "easy to be entreated" instead of "willing to yield." Notice that when God's leading you, it brings peace. When God's leading you, it's just pure. There's no hypocrisy in it. You're committed because you know that this lines up with the Word and you've got the witness in your spirit. Now your faith can operate because you've got full conviction in your heart that God's going to get you there.

I always tell everybody this, you will know if God's leading you to do something if you follow peace. The Holy Spirit will always lead you into peace. The first thing the Lord will do in your life is bring you into peace. If you haven't found peace, you haven't gotten into God's will yet and you're not in faith yet because when you get into faith, peace comes into your heart.

"For we who have believed do enter that rest."
Hebrews 4:3 (NKJV)

That tells me the moment I really am believing, a rest or a peace begins to come into me. I have a confidence in God that I'm going to make it. The circumstances may still be just as bad. The symptoms may be just as bad. The attack may be just as bad, but I've heard from God. I have a peace and I have a conviction that God's going to get me through. Now I've got wisdom operating in me. Now my faith will work because I know the Lord's in this with me. I know I'm going to get to the other side. God's going to get me there.

In verse 18, James says those who make peace sow in peace and grow the fruit of righteousness. In other words, if I'm going to produce, I'm going to do it through peace. I'm going to follow God. He's going to show me the way to get there.

Everything doesn't just happen. You don't always just hear what God wants you to do in just a few minutes of seeking Him. Sometimes it takes a little bit of time in His presence to really lock down on what He's saying to you. There are no shortcuts. The trouble with us being led by the Spirit and using our faith is this: We want to pray a five second prayer, get an answer from God, and get up and go about doing what we want to do. Sometimes you don't receive direction because you aren't able to hear from God. Your mind can talk to you all day long and your head can still roar with all the problems and the thoughts at the end of the day. You might say you're going to bed early, but at one o'clock in the morning, your mind is still running with all the stuff going on. It's sometimes easier to get your body quiet than it is to get your head quiet. All these voices, all the worry, all the anxiety: with all this stuff going on, you can't hear God. Sometimes the reason we're not getting direction is because we haven't taken time to get ourselves in a position to be able to hear the voice of our Shepherd.

So many times we want to ask others to pray for us to hear from God. You can't do that. It's just tossing the responsibility off on somebody else. Or we want to do like Gideon. We want to do a fleece here to see God's will. But you're about to get messed up if you do that because the Bible doesn't say, As many as are led by *fleeces* are sons of God. It says in Romans 8:14, "As many as are led by the Spirit." You have to get yourself to the place where you're hearing what God wants you to do. God is going to show you how to use your faith and the path you're supposed to follow. Your faith will not work if you fall on the wrong path. Sometimes we have to get ourselves quiet and get ourselves in position for the anointing to flow and for the will of God to be done and we can hear God's voice.

In Isaiah 40, God speaks through the prophet Isaiah:

> "Have you not known?
> Have you not heard?
> The everlasting God, the LORD,
> The Creator of the ends of the earth,
> Neither faints nor is weary.
> His understanding is unsearchable.
> He gives power to the weak,
> And to *those who have* no might He increases strength.
> Even the youths shall faint and be weary,
> And the young men shall utterly fall,
> But those who wait on the LORD
> Shall renew *their* strength;

> They shall mount up with wings like eagles,
> They shall run and not be weary,
> They shall walk and not faint."

Isaiah 40:28-31 (NKJV)

Notice that it says those who wait upon the Lord, those who seek the Lord diligently. Those who call out to the Lord, those who spend time in His presence. That word wait in the Hebrew means to bind together. Those who take enough time to come in oneness with the Lord. They get their strength renewed, soar like eagles and run without getting tired. Because they have taken time to be able to hear God's voice.

For instance, I was pastoring the first little church I was in, and we'd been there about three years. I knew that it was time for change to take place. I prayed and I just couldn't get down what the Lord wanted me to do. It's the first time I'm having to make this kind of change. The first time the Lord had led me to come to this church in a very supernatural way. This time I hadn't heard any thunder or lightning or anything spectacular, but I knew He was wanting me to do something. I just didn't know what to do.

I told Bonnie I was going to go and get in the presence of the Lord. We lived in a little parsonage but I said I was going to be in the living room. I was just going to pray and wait on the Lord and minister to the Lord. I had to hear what God wanted me to do. It was evening when I started in the

89

presence of the Lord. About nine o'clock the next morning, I was just lying there and just praying a little bit in the Spirit and worshiping God, as Acts 13:2 says. I quit crying and asking God what to do and just began ministering to Him, worshiping Him, thanking and praising Him. My mind got quiet and my spirit got connected with Him.

To wait upon the Lord means to bind together. I made my connection, and all of a sudden, the Spirit of the Lord spoke to me—the Lord Himself through the Holy Spirit spoke to me. It was so loud. It was like He was yelling, and He was telling me the next step and where I was to go, what I was to do, and the choices I would have to make. One would be an easier one, but it would not take me as far as the other. One would be hard, but it would launch my ministry farther. He said, "I will let you go both ways, but you have to choose. I won't make the choice for you, but I'll bless you in whichever way. I can bless you more if you do this one, but it will be harder." I was listening to Him, but it sounded like He was yelling. Finally, I said, "Lord, why are you yelling at me?" The Lord said this, and I never forgot it, He said, "I'm not yelling. This is my normal volume of speech. You just finally got yourself cleaned up enough to be able to hear Me without all the static."

Sometimes we've got to clean out the static of all the other voices. We've got to clean out all of the other junk to be able to hear clearly and precisely the voice of the Lord to know what we're supposed to do. There are no shortcuts. That's where the Church as a whole today is missing it because we live in an instant culture. Sometimes to be renewed and to find the will of God and know the way of God, it takes us doing some separation. We need to turn off the TV, turn off the phone, turn off Facebook and other distractions. We need to get into the Word and begin praying, worshiping and ministering to the Lord until we can clearly hear the voice of God speak to us.

Then the Lord spoke this to me: "Son, I have been saying this to you for the last couple of weeks. It's not me that's been quiet. It's you that's not been able to hear. You finally got desperate enough in your heart, knowing that you weren't able to hear, that you pressed in." That was in 1980.

I'd like to say that I pressed in every time. Unfortunately, I've not been that smart every time. I've often tried to do it on my own. Pray a quick prayer. Believe God and speak a word, but it didn't work. I've finally come to the place where I said, "Lord, I'm missing it somewhere. I'm not making connection here now. You're not the problem. I'm the problem. So I'm going to spend time in your presence until I hear you telling me what I'm supposed to do." I already knew that it's His will to bless me in everything I do. He said in Deuteronomy 28:8, He would bless everything I put my hand to. But I need to know what He wants me to put my hand to.

Every time I've taken time to wait upon the Lord, minister to the Lord, and spend time in His presence until I heard in my heart the way to do it, I've gotten victory. Even though I started messing it up by not doing it right, the Lord did not come in and condemn me. He just came in and said, "Now, listen, you could have had this done a lot quicker, but let me show you how to fix it." God never comes in and condemns. God comes in and helps correct and straighten it up and get it right.

If you've been painting your room the wrong color, the Lord comes in and says that's the wrong color. He'll help you get the right color. Then He'll help you cover up the paint that you already put on the wall so it looks right when it's done. The Holy Spirit Himself is our helper. He's the one that gets involved with us. When you can come to that place, your faith will not fail.

Just how bad do you want the help? Do you want it bad enough to spend some time when you're faint, when you're weary, when you can't run, or when you can't walk another step? Are you willing to back off, turn everything off, get with God in prayer and say, "Lord, I'm going to wait on you until you show me your will and show me your way to do it." If you will do this, your faith will come alive and you'll walk in victory. Then you'll believe, and you'll speak, and you will have God's will working in your life.

CPSIA information can be obtained
at www.ICGtesting.com
Printed in the USA
JSHW040425220922
30841JS00001B/6